HOW TO MAKE

LOVE

THE SECRET OF WOOING AND WINNING
THE ONE YOU LOVE

ISBN: 0-9786649-0-6

CONTENTS

CONTENTS

FOREWORD

When the first man looked upon the first woman and was satisfied with her, that was when love began. And that was millions of years ago, if we are to believe our scientists. So it may seem that this book is unnecessary considering the aeons that man has been making love. But, as in everything, man has seldom profited from his experiences of the past. He has fought thousands of wars to no good purpose and he will continue to fight wars to the same reason. Once on the sucker lists of a stockmarket manipulator, he will continue to buy worthless stocks. And even after he has been burned by a flame, he will continue to stick his finger into the candle-flame. Therefore, although he has been making love for centuries, the art of love as it should be practiced continues to be unknown to him. Perhaps it has been because of our Puritan upbringing. However, the fact remains that some guide is necessary to insure a happy love affair.

True, in the past fifty years, there have been some attempts made to publish books on the art of love. But a perusal of them will uncover the fact that, although we live in a modern age, we seem unable to throw off the yoke of Puritanism. In the main, these books concerned themselves with the language of flowers as practiced between lovers, the language of fans, the language of parasols and, in fact treatises on the symbolic language of everything but the language of love.

What has been vitally necessary is a book written by a modern writer for modern people who live and love in a modern way. The restrictions that bound us in the past, in the matter of social etiquette, have all been washed away by the cleansing waters of time. Not many years ago, our girls were warned to keep their young men from placing their arms around the seat of the buggy when riding or else suffer the ignominy of being classed as fallen women. Nowadays, we look upon such things more calmly. With the change in social customs there has been a need for a book which dealt with the art of love. This book is intended to aid you in your love-making.

PIETRO RAMIREZ

Different Ways of Meeting Your Mate

WHAT IS LOVE?

First we must understand what love is. Once we understand the meaning of love, then we can practice it more perfectly. Love has been, perhaps, the most widely used theme of our poets and they have defined love in many ways. Pope, for instance, says that love is a disease. Greenville said that love was a plant. Bulwer said it was a loadstone. Shakespeare said that love was blind. Ovid said that love is the perpetual source of fears and anxieties. At another time, this famous poetic lover said that love was an affair of credulity. And Longfellow said that love was the root of creation. Other poets have said that love is heaven, love is master, love is a feast and love is love.

Longfellow, it seems, came closer to the true definition of love when he said that "Love is the root of creation: God's essence." For love, if it is to be the true kind of love, should always be directed to eventual creation, that is to say, to the creation of children in the married state.

Marriage is the culmination of love. Two people should never fall in love with each other unless they understand thoroughly that their love for each other is to eventuate into a future marriage. Our civilization has lasted as long as it has because we have adhered strictly to this system of the relationship between man and woman. The birth of a child demands that man and woman participate in the creation. This is what marriage means: a coming together, a comingling, a fluxing, a joining, all for the purpose of perpetuating the race. This drive in the human being to perpetuate his race is blind. We do it only because something within us forces us to do it. And it is that same blind something that brings two people together neither knowing the why of their communion but each feeling that the marriage of their two selves was inevitable.

It is this blind drive, this unknown force of magnetism that attracts them to each other, that is love. And love is life. Without love we would not have marriage. Without marriage we would have children, perhaps, but the family which is only possible in the marriage state would not exist and the family has been the sole reason for the perpetuation of civilization and the perpetuation of life itself. Therefore, you can see how we get the saying that it's love that makes the world go round.

What we must remember, though, is that although it is nature that creates a mutual love in two people, it is the two people, themselves, who are responsible for the continuation of that love. Omar Khayyam said that only a hair divides the false and true. He could have said that even less than a hair divides love and hate. It takes very little for a great love to be changed into a great hate. Therefore, a working knowledge of the art of love is absolutely essential to the young couple who have ventured into love in order for that love to be perpetuated.

It is this knowledge of the art of love that this book intends to explain in the follow pages.

MAN AND WOMAN HE CREATED THEM

Before going into a discussion of the art of love, it is necessary that we understand the basic foundation on which love rests. There is only one kind of love and that is the love of a man for a woman or vice versa. Mother love, brother love, sister love, Platonic love, even the "unspeakable loves" of Oscar Wilde and Lord Alfred Douglas and Lesbia and her charming girls on the isle of Paphos, none of these is true love.

Man and woman; He created them.

Man was created strong. Woman was created weak. Therefore, it is up to man to protect his woman. Woman is so physically constituted that she needs man's strong protection. It is she who has the onus of bearing the children. While in this condition, she naturally is unable to protect herself. That is one of the parts that man plays in the drama of the creation of life. Even the supposed unthinking animals realize this. Consider the watchful lion holding guard over his lioness mate while she suckles her cubs. Consider even the chirping jaybird who peeps ominously at an intruder of the nest in which his mate is hatching her eggs and flutters his wings threateningly at any who dare assail his family.

Man Was Created Strong

With that as a basis, we can readily understand the differences between man and woman. For instance there is the difference in the attitude of man and woman toward the culmination of love. Woman, although she is just as anxious for love as man, must never betray her anxiety. She must always be passive. Man, it is, who must be the active partner. It is he who makes love to woman. He chases the woman who was made to be chased. The success of love depends entirely on the understanding of this basic relationship.

From this we understand why man must be tender towards his woman. It is this same tenderness which evidences his care over her welfare and confesses his wardship as his woman's protector. Victor Hugo once wrote that "the most powerful symptom of love is a tenderness which at times becomes almost insupportable."

Therefore, it is because man is the active half in an affair of love that this book is directed mostly to him. But woman should also understand these principles that make tor the success of love and, with her cooperation, aid her man in making this active-passive, chaser-chased, strong-weak relationship possible. That accounts for woman's coyness, her shyness. That also accounts for her sometimes illogical habits of putting her man off. She realizes intuitively that, in order to make herself more desirable to her man, she must make herself less accessible. She must, in other words, establish the chaser-chased relationship between them. She knows as Meade, the writer, knew that "a lover is like a hunter—if the game begot with too much ease he cares not for't." In plain English, the easier it is to get the less we want a thing.

The time when Sir Walter Raleigh laid his fine cloak into the mud for Queen Elizabeth was more a gesture of love than it was a gesture of loyalty from a subject to his queen. He was merely exhibiting his regard for the welfare of the woman he loves. Nowadays, a man would seize hold of his girlfriend and carry her over the muddy pond and he would, in this way, demonstrate his strength and the use he makes of it to take care of his weaker mate. The old custom of a bridegroom's carrying his bride across the threshold of their new home is another example of this display of strength on the part of the male as it evidences itself with his wife who might be, in real-ity, a buxom wench as strong, perhaps, as her bridegroom. But the custom realizes the basic necessity of establishing this strong-weak relationship as soon as possible, therefore the continuation of it.

Sir Walter Raleigh's Gesture of Love

A reversed relationship, that is where the woman is the physical superior of the man, is not only devoid of love but is ludicrous. That's why such comics as Barney Google and his enormous wife were funny. That's why Jiggs is so humorous because Mrs. Jiggs lords it over Jiggs, throws vases at him and makes him the weaker part of their marital relationship. If the strong-weak attitude between man and woman is kept up throughout the entire period of lovemaking, courtship and marriage, the result will be a happy marriage that will bear fruit in love, children and marital bliss.

LOVE AT FIRST SIGHT

One of the arguments about love which has never been solved is the question of love at first sight. One school of thought insists that love at first sight is not lasting. The other says it is the only kind of love. Marlowe, for instance, writes "Whoever loved that loved not at sight." This, however, is futile argument. The question is not when does love start but how long will it last? And the object of all lovers is to see to

Love At First Sight

it that love lasts forever and ever. Longfellow, perhaps, hit it right when he wrote: "It is difficult to know at what moment love begins; it is less difficult to know it has begun. A thousand heralds proclaim it to the listening ear, a thousand messengers betray it to the eye. Tone, act, attitude and look, the signals upon the countenance, the electric telegraph of touch," all of these are indications of the beginning of a great love.

Thousands of young men and women have grown up together in friendship only. They made mud pies together in their babyhood. They went to grammar school together. The young man carried the young girl's books home from high school. All of this they did without knowing why they did it. Suddenly, at a picnic in the forest preserves, after they had deserted the throng of other picnickers and found a lonely spot in the shade near a tinkling brook, the boy looked up into the girl's eyes and he sees something in them that he had never seen before. A strange sparkle is there. He feels a catch come to his throat. A delicious sensation pervades his whole body. His breath seems to come in short gasps. He sees that the same reactions have come to the girl. He sees her bosom heave. He sees her avert her eyes in embarrassment. He knows, she knows, they both know that love has suddenly come to them. And although they cannot identify it as love, they know that it is something that is sweet, something that is so overpowering in its strength that its sweetness is almost pain. Then it is that love is born.

Surely, we cannot say that this is not true love because it is not love at first sight. Perhaps it is a truer love than love at first sight. Certainly, it is a love that should prove more lasting. For, throughout those previous years, they have learned to know each other intimately. They know each other's faults and vices. They know each other's little idiosyncrasies, those same little idiosyncrasies that have broken up what was once a happy love life. And it is in the understanding of each other that true love is born and nurtures and lives.

LOVE IS A COMMON SYMPATHY

For that is the secret of a lasting love, the one word: understanding. Only when there is this understanding, this common sympathy for each other, can true love function. The man must understand thoroughly the reasons for his loved one's strange actions at times. He must understand that his lover has her qualities which make her beloved to him and, being human, she also has her faults. It is understanding these faults and making the necessary allowances for them that make for a long love life. Similarly, the girl must understand the characteristics of her man which make him human. She must realize that, sometimes, he would like to be alone. And she sees to it that she is not always in his way. If he clicks his teeth while he eats the morning toast, with her understanding of this, she does not allow it to get on her nerves and thus foster a dislike not only for the fault but also for the man, but she says to herself resignedly, "Oh well, that's John's way of eating and nothing will make him change." That is understanding. That is love.

So it can be seen that the love which grows out of a long friendship is more desired than the love which is generated suddenly at first sight. If, after the sudden burst of first love, the lovers realize that they must learn to know each other thoroughly and they go about learning each other, then their love will be lasting. But, experience has proven that, usually, those lovers who are catapulted into a lover affair at first sight are usually those who are quick-tempered. A hair-trigger emotion such as love at first sight can only be possessed by people with hair-trigger temperaments. Such people haven't the faculty for logical reasoning. Seldom, are they able to say to each other calmly and dispassionately, "Let's sit down and know ourselves." Instead, they fly into a love affair, imbibe hastily of the sweets of love, nibble speedily of the little tidbits and, as fast as they have flown into love, fly out of it. Love which is the culmination of a long friendship is not actuated by a hair-trigger. It sits down at the banquet of love slowly; it partakes of the hors d'oeuvres, the soup, the main course, all of the side dishes, everything including dessert. It enjoys to the fullest extent Ovid's "Banquet of Love."

WHEN ARE YOU IN LOVE?

There is one difficulty that besets a young person who seeks for love. Like the gold-miner who comes across a large lode of quartz streaked with a substance that looks like gold but which later, on assay, turns out to be iron pyrites or "fool's gold," the lover is apt to come across a girl with whom he thinks he is in love but who later turns out to be only another person. This is only an infatuation. It is a sudden flaring up of love and a sudden dying down of it. The trouble is that its symptoms are exactly the same as true love. The same catch in the throat, the same aching void in the heart in an absence, the same overwhelming surge to the lover, the same passionate responses in an embrace and a kiss are present in an infatuation as are in true love. The only difference comes not in the quality but in the time consumed. Where an infatuation is a matter of the minute, true love is a matter of a lifetime. Yet, how are we to tell the difference between an infatuation and true love at the onset of the love affair? Some people react to disillusioning infatuations healthily. They allow them to roll off their backs, forget them immediately and go on in the search for true love. Others, more sensitive than the rest, brood disconsolately over the loss of what they thought was true love, become hypochondriacs and suffer torture and agony. Oftimes, they allow their sorrow to prevent them ever from loving again. That, in most cases, accounts for our multitudes of bachelors and spinsters. At some time in their lives, they allowed themselves to succumb to an infatuation, fell away from it and grieved for the rest of their lives, vowing that they would never be caught in the same situation and swearing off the opposite sex entirely, the while they treasured, in memory, the picture of their first great love who disillusioned them. How, then, are we to know what is infatuation and what is true love?

GROW UP WITH EACH OTHER

One way of avoiding this is by growing up with each other, learning to know each other and growing together through the years in a friendship which will, inevitably, blossom into love. But all of us are not given that opportunity. Most of us rarely settle down in one place for a long period of years, long enough at least to begin a friendship with a future lover. We must seek for love "on the jump" as it were. There is but one solution to this important problem and that is an attempt at a common understanding. You must sit down with yourself, alone and start a conversation with yourself. First you must forget entirely about love. You must strip away everything romantic about your affair with the person with whom you think yourself to be in love. Bring your love down to earth. Then, when you have done this, ask yourself these questions:

> Can he take care of me after marriage?
> What are his faults?
> Can I tolerate those faults?
> What are his virtues?
> Do the virtues compensate for his faults?

Frankly, few people are strong minded enough to divorce themselves entirely from love. They will not answer these questions truthfully. They will say to themselves, "Oh, what do I care if he takes a bath only on Saturday night, I love him and I'm happy only when I'm with him." It is such as they who fling themselves headlong into a love affair, come to the realization that they cannot stand the sweaty odor day after day and eventually end up in the divorce courts. This treatise on the art of love was written only to direct the way. It cannot force people into the right path. And people, being what they are, will follow the dictates of their hearts rather than their brains. They will suffer. They will be burned. Some of them will come out unhurt. While others will emerge from a lost love embittered, soul-scarred and cursing love, love which they really never experienced.

ANOTHER PRELIMINARY TO LOVE

"True love never runs smooth" is an old saying which can be attributed mostly to the fact that the parents of both parties are interfering in the love relationship. Now I don't mean to say that parents should not interfere. After all, they have spent a goodly number of years in bringing up their children and they want to be certain that their child will be happy in love. Naturally, they are desirous of passing on the lover, on determining for their own satisfaction that the boy or the girl who is in love with their child is worthy. They also feel that, with their own experience of love, courtship and marriage, they should be able to advise their child and direct his or her way through its love life. This, however, is wrong. These parents should realize that love cannot be guided by anyone but those in love. Love is entirely irrational. And, what is more, love is peculiarly perverse. The more you discourage love in a person the more that person will adhere to it. Many girls have married lovers whom they would have turned down after the infatuation had worn off had they been let alone by their parents. But the more the parents nagged, the firmer was the belief of the girls that their lovers were ideals. When they saw their lovers being jumped on by their parents, there was naturally created in them a feeling of sympathy for their lovers. And sympathy engenders love, even though it is a shortlived love. And the natural result is a throwing of oneself into a disastrous marriage if only to spite your parents.

There is only one way to avoid such disagreeable situations. Always, always insist that, at some early time in the love affair, the parents of both lovers meet the lovers. If your loved one refuses to meet your parents, then your first suspicion should be that, for some reason or other, he is afraid to meet them. Think out a possible reason for this fear. And demand one of your lover. If his reason is illogical and shifty, drop him immediately. He is out for no good. If, however, his reason is reasonable, explain to him the circumstance surrounding you and your home life. Tell him that if your affair is to continue happily, it is essential that your parents meet him. If he loves you as you think he does, he will overcome any objection he might have, if only to make you happy. That should be a proof of his love for you and should, in itself, be indicative of his intentions toward you. Once your parents have approved of your lover, then there will be no chance of arguments, bickering and nagging. Your way will be clear in front of you to a happy, blissful love life. The highroad to love will be straight ahead of you leading to the passionate hours of true love.

Introduce Your Lover to
Your Parents

LOVE, LOVE

Now starts the art of making love. We have gone through the preliminaries necessary to the understanding of the basis of the continuation of true love so as to insure you that your love will continue. Now to continue with love.

First, you must always remember that tenderness for each other is one of the surest signs of true love, Every effort should be made to be tender to each other. There are a hundred different ways of doing little things for each other in which you can be tender. An absolute remembering of each other's birthdays, for instance, is one way. Exchanging books is another way. Showing an interest in each other's parents goes a long way in establishing a bond between the lovers. Oh, there are thousands of ways, little ways to be sure, with which you can show your concern over the comfort and welfare of the person you love. And they should always be practiced, always. A lapse in tenderness can only be interpreted as a lapse in love.

THE FIRST KISS

Time was, in the Victorian days, when a kiss was the holy of holies to a couple in love. Only after months and months of friendship was the first kiss ever indulged in. A girl would think it an affront to her honor to be kissed before then. And a young man would never dare "insult" his lover by suggesting such a thing for fear he might lose her forever. But things have changed in that regard. Nowadays, a kiss is a matter of fact thing between two people who have met each other and who feel that they are, or are going to be, in love.

At this time, then, it should be quite appropriate to quote from our book, *The Art of Kissing*, in order to explain how the first kiss of a pair of lovers should be accomplished. And, this first kiss is important for it will foretell the kind of lover that you are going to be and show that you either "know your stuff" or are just another inept boor.

HOW TO APPROACH A GIRL

In kissing a girl whose experience with osculation is limited, it is a good thing to work up to the kissing of the lips. Only an arrant fool seizes hold of such a girl when they are comfortably seated on a sofa, and suddenly shoves his face into hers and smacks her lips. Naturally, the first thing he should do is to arrange it so that the girl is seated against the arm of the sofa while he is at her side. In this way, she cannot edge away from him when he becomes serious in his attentions. This done, on some pretext or other, such as a gallant attempt to adjust the cushions behind her (tenderness, you see) he manages to insinuate his arm, first around the back of the sofa and then, gradually, around her shoulders.

If she flinches, don't worry. If she flinches and makes an outcry, don't worry. If she flinches, makes an outcry and tries to get up from the sofa, don't worry. Hold her, gently but firmly, and allay her fears with kind, reassuring words. Remember what Shakespeare said about "a woman's no." However, if she flinches, makes an outcry, a loud stentorian outcry, mind you, and starts to scratch your face, then start to worry or start to get yourself out of a bad situation. Such girls are not to be trifled with... or kissed. It is such as they, in most cases, who still believe the story of the stork which brings babies because of the consequences of a kiss.

But if your arm is comfortably reposed across the girl's shoulders and "all's right with the world," then your next step is to flatter her in some way. All women like to be flattered. They like to be told they are beautiful even when the mirror throws the lie back into their ugly faces.

Flatter her!

Catullus once wrote:

> *Kiss me softly and speak to me low;*
> *Trust me darling, the time is near,*
> *When we may live with never a fear*
> *Kiss me dear!*
> *Kiss me softly, and speak to me low!*

Tell her she is beautiful. Then take a deep sniff of the perfume in her hair and comment on it. Tell her that the odor is like "heady wine." Tell her that her hair smells like a garden of roses. Tell her anything, but be sure to tell her something complimentary. This done, it is only a natural thing for you to desire to sink your nose deeper into her hair so that you can get the full benefit of its bouquet.

THE TECHNIQUE OF KISSING

Now is your chance! The moment you feel the tip of your nose touch her scalp, purse your lips and kiss her, the while you inhale a deep breath of air that is redolent with the exquisite odor of her hair. It is then but a few inches to her ear. Touch the rim of her ear with your lips in a sort of brushing motion. Breathe gently into the delicate shell. Some women react passionately to this subtle act. Brush past her here in this way again and note her reaction. If she draws her head away, return to the hair and sniff luxuriously of it. Then settle back to her ear, the while you murmur "sweet, airy nothings" into it. From the ear to her neck is but another few inches. Let your lips traverse this distance quickly and then dart into the nape of the neck and, with your lips well pursed, nip the skin there, using the same gentleness as would a cat lifting her precious kittens.

Then, with a series of little nips, bring your lips around from the nape of her neck to the curving, swerve of her jaw, close to the ear. Gently kiss the lobe of her ear. But be sure to return to the tender softness of her jaw. From then on, the way should be clear to you. Nuzzle your lips along the soft, downy expanse until you reach the corner of her lips. You will know when this happens, because, suddenly, you will feel a strange stiffening of her shoulders under your arm. The reason for this is that the lips constitute one of the main erogenous zones of the body.

All right. You have subtly kissed the corner of her mouth. Don't hesitate. Push on further to more pleasurable spots. Ahead of you lies that which had been promised in your dreams, the tender, luscious lips of the girl you love. But don't sit idly by and watch them quivering.

Act!

Lift your lips away slightly, center them so that when you make contact there will be a perfect union. Notice, only momentarily, the picture of her teeth in her lips, and, then, like a seagull swooping gracefully down through the air, bring your lips down firmly onto the lips of the girl who is quivering in your arms.

Kiss her!

Kiss her as though, at that moment, nothing else exists in the world. Kiss her as though your entire life is wrapped up into the period of the kiss. Kiss her as though there is nothing else that you would rather be doing. Kiss her!

AND MORE LOVE

Of course, this sort of kissing cannot be indulged in everywhere. But there are dozens of places and situations where little nips of kisses can be stolen surreptitiously. At the theatre, for instance. When attending a drama or a musical comedy, never under any circumstances, put your arm around your girl or attempt any obvious intimacies. Be satisfied with holding her hand well down between the seats or in her lap. There is a delicious little game that can be played in this fashion by entwining your fingers in hers time and time again or rubbing your fingers together. Too, the touch of your shoulders can accomplish wonders in their proximity. For, it is not always necessary that you contact her with your lips. Body contact is sometimes as delicious because it withholds the fulfillment and dangles the fruit of joy out of reach and thus makes it all the more enjoyable once it is attained.

In a moving picture theatre, it is an entirely different thing. The formality of the dramatic theatre is not present here. And, if both you and your loved one are so disposed, it is entirely correct for you to put your arm around her shoulders and squeeze them whenever the occasion calls for it... which should be quite often. Then, you can also use your free hand to hold her hand which you can squeeze or fondle or use to entwine in her fingers. But, of course, you should never be too promiscuous. When in the movie or in public, your lovemaking should be as inconspicuous as possible. In the first place, it isn't good taste. And, in the second place, it isn't fair to the

Right and Wrong at the Theatre

girl to put her into such an embarrassing position, if she is in any way feminine and therefore sensitive to such vulgar displays of love. This should be another way to demonstrate tenderness and regard for her feelings and should be an indication of your love for her. "All the world loves a lover" is an old saying but, when the world sees lovemaking in the open, it becomes morbidly curious and, sometimes, it laughs or giggles and that is embarrassing to anyone and is liable to deaden the most ardent of passions in a girl for a boy.

THE OBJECT OF LOVE

One thing you must always remember: love, all love builds for future happiness. And this future happiness is a successful marriage. Nothing should be done in this pre-marital state that might injure the marriage relationship. Remember that ahead of you lies a life together, a life that will be built on a happy home, healthy children, congenial companionship and, above all, loyalty. And, always, in the back of your head, while you are courting, while you are kissing, while you are fondling each other, while you are enjoying each other, you should have the thought of this idea of building for permanence.

For instance, while the affair is still young, only the most innocent of kisses is permissible. Lip kisses, cheek kisses, neck kisses, hair kisses, hand kisses, all of these are perfectly proper because, in themselves, they are enjoyable and lead up to nothing of a more serious nature. However, it is the various other kisses, the more intimate kisses, the more intimate fondlings and endearments that should be stringently avoided during this period. For they lead to things which should be avoided like the plague. Young blood is hot blood and if it is stirred by "soul" kisses and other such dangerous pastimes, the consequences might be regretable. Remember that, in a short while, there will be a time and place for that sort of thing. You will get enough of passionate kissing when you are entitled to it. For, as Stanislaus has said, "Love weakens as it grows older, while friendship strengthens with the years." And that is what you should be building for constantly, after love, the physical love, has left you in your later years, friendship, an eternal, lasting friendship and companionship. And these are only possible if you withhold the passions that seethe within you and reserve them for the proper time.

After you have reached a marriage understanding, then is the time for the more intimate forms of kissing. These forms are gone into in detail in the author's book, *The Art of Kissing*, and a perusal of its contents should lead the way to an enjoyment of that most satisfying of arts, that most joyful of pleasures, that most excruciating of delectable tortures... kissing.

HOW DOES LOVE SPEAK?

In the wild words that uttered seem so weak
They shrink ashamed to silence; in the fire
Glance strikes with glance, swift flashing higher and higher,
Like lightings that precede the mighty storm;
In the deep, soulful stillness; in the warm,

> *Impassioned tide that sweeps through the throbbing veins,*
> *Between the shores of deep delights and pains;*
> *In the embrace where madness melts in bliss,*
> *And in the convulsive rapture, of a kiss—*
>   *Thus doth love speak.*

But a word of caution. Here, as before, the same care should be taken about "going too far." You are still not ready for the culmination of love: connubial bliss. You are still in the testing ground of love and you should steel yourself and your emotions until the proper time is at hand. The writer, Calton, has put this thought pithily into a sentence when he said "Love is an alliance of friendship and animalism; if the former predominate, it is a passion exalted and refined; but if the latter, gross and sensual." Be refined and exalted in your pre-marital kisses and endearments and not gross and sensual. Remember what the poet wrote when he said:

> *A necklace of love for my lady*
> *That was linked by the angels above—*
> *No other but this—and the tender, sweet kiss*
> *That sealeth a little one's love.*

The moral of this poem is in the phrase "the tender sweet kiss." And that is what all your kisses should be before they are entitled to be anything else, "tender and sweet." Keep this in mind and you will discover that, when you have the privilege of the other kisses, they will be sweeter and blissful and infinitely more passionate. For, then, you will be first experiencing the bliss of the passion kiss, experiencing it when it can eventuate into what it should be, the deep-seated, passionate, soul-stirring kiss of married life.

HOW TO KEEP LOVE

Having attained love, the question becomes how can you keep it? Many a love affair that started with a blaze of glory ends up with a fizzle of despair. And, mind you, the breakup was not because the lovers were unsuited for each other but because one of them was negligent in her duty to herself as a lover to keep herself either physically or mentally attractive. Oh yes, it's quite possible to be mentally attractive, too. You may doll yourself up with the most expensive of "warpaint," you may be a reincarnation of Helen of Troy, Cleopatra and the Venus de Milo but, in some cases, this will not avail you if you are not, likewise, mentally attractive. By this I mean that you should develop your mind in such a way so that it corresponds to the mind of your lover. It isn't necessary for you to go to college to do this. All you have to do is to study your lover and adjust your actions and your thoughts so that they blend in perfectly with him. And that is what all love is: a blending of self, both physically and mentally, a fluxing of he and she, a, fluid, even, coming together of the two sexes.

I LIKE WHAT YOU LIKE

For instance, you should see to it that you have common interests. That is, you must adjust your life so that you learn to like the things your lover likes, whether it be books, radio programs, friends or even orchestra leaders. That is why a love affair between two young people who have lived together for many years is invariably successful. They have come to learn each other's likes and dislikes and, through the years, have adjusted each other's tastes to suit them.

BE TRUE MY HEART

Another pre-requisite that makes for a continuation of love is loyalty. This is all important because, so often, we are tempted to flirt with the first athlete who comes along, just to see if our flirting apparatus is still in good working order. Just an innocent flirtation, you know. But those innocent flirtations can have their serious consequences. Not only can the flirt involve herself in an unwanted love affair but she can just as quickly disattach herself from a desirable love affair. And you can be loyal to your lover not only in deeds but in thoughts as well. In other words, if you are truly in love with a person, you see no evil that he does, you hear of no evil that he has done, and you speak of no evil that he might have done. You rest back calmly and say to yourself, "I am loyal to Joe, because I love him and, if he has really done something that he shouldn't have done then he will come to me and tell me about it because he loves me." By this, I don't mean to say that, like the ostrich, you should sink your head into the sand and hide yourself from realities. No, certainly not that. But, where there is the slightest doubt about anything, where there is no absolute proof then your loyalty should always be with your loved one and no doubts should enter your mind until definite, absolute proof is offered. Even then, I would doubt what has been said until I have corroborated it from the lips of my lover. After that, I would try to understand him and that would be another way of preserving love.

TO ERR IS HUMAN

Understanding your lover is something that is required of you if your love affair is to continue to marriage. Realize that no one is perfect and that each of us is likely to err. If the faults irritate you, remember, try to remember the things about your lover that have made him so lovable to you. Balance off the bad with the good. See the big things only and let the little things go hang. Or else, if you discover some shortcomings in your lover that disturb you, think back on your own shortcomings and realize that, the things about him that are annoying to you are just as bad as the things about you that are annoying to him. Then go about adjusting those annoyances of yours and, pretty soon, if your loved one is the least observant and is actually in love with you, he will realize what you are trying to do and will see to it, that the petty things that he does will be done away with.

CLEAN LIVING

One of the most annoying things that can disrupt a love affair is personal uncleanliness. If you are a girl, see to it that everything you wear is fresh and clean and free from any objectionable odors. Tub yourself continually in hot water and use cold water and soap to cleanse your skin so that it will always be alluring and attractive. If you are a young man, then you, too, should always be fresh-looking. You don't

have to be a Beau Brummel to do this. All you need do is be
clean. Take frequent showers or tubs; keep your nails clean
if not manicured; see that your suits are attended to. Be well
groomed and you will be a groom sure enough.

THE SECRET OF SUZANNE

Again, hold no secrets from your lover. After all, you are
both bound for a relationship which will be so intimate,
so revealing that not one iota of your life should be con-
cealed from your partner. For you never can tell when that
secret may be revealed. And, with the revelation will come
a denouement that might break up what was, before the
incident, a happy love life. Hide nothing from your lover. Tell
him everything, your secret desires, your hopes, your faults,
your failures, everything. A sure indication of love is the tell-
ing of something which has been secret to you and you alone.
And if your loved one is appreciative, he will understand
and make the necessary allowances and, together, stand-
ing shoulder to shoulder, you can fight the thing out and
conquer it. Secrets are horrible things. Hidden, they fester
and gnaw like canker worms until they become unbearable.
Brought out to the light, they die quickly and the chance
of their being obliterated entirely is more certain than if
they were allowed to remain secrets, aching foreboding and
always ready to leap into action and disrupt your happiness.
The only way to fight a secret is to uncover it.

WHEN LOVE LIES LOVE DIES

Similarly, the worst thing you could do to a love is to lie to your lover. No matter how small the lie may be, it is likely to come back and trip you up. If you are a man, don't lie about your salary. Don't try to make yourself more wealthy than you actually are. Your real worth will come out in the long run if you intend to marry the girl, as all true lovers should. So why start your love life out under false colors? You only delay the time when you will have to come forth with the truth and the truth, sometimes, can be so bitter a pill to swallow as to break up an affair that would have otherwise been a happy and long lived life of bliss. If you are old, then your age, if it is not too disproportionate, means nothing to love. A few years leeway between lovers make no difference. Whatever you do, don't try to trick your lover into a love affair. You might be able to get away with it for a time. But, eventually, those things have a way of getting out and the result is embarrassment and, what is more likely, the end of things.

GEE! YOU'RE A SWELL KID

Another excellent method of prolonging a love affair, is to be appreciative. You know the abilities of your loved one and, when those abilities should be praised, then praise them. It really doesn't matter how trifling those capabilities are. It may be that the girlfriend has made a pan of fudge for you. Be appreciative of it. Tell her that it certainly is the best fudge you ever tasted. People are funny. They like to be praised even if the thing they are praised for is inconsequential. So praise her or him. If her nose is a little gem of creation, tell her so. If your John is handy with tools around the house, then tell him so. Mention it to your friends, sometimes. Give John a chance to swell up with a little pride. It's those little things that go a long way to cementing your love-life.

LOVE IS NOT A PRISON SENTENCE

Now comes a most important injunction to further love. Respect the independence of your loved one. Remember that it is very easy to become satiated with fine foods. Once in awhile, instead of truffles and lobsters, you crave a hunk of juicy homemade apple-pie. And the same applies to love. Your lover does not want to be in your company, every minute of the day, every day of the year, every year of his life. Don't depend on him to be ready always to take you to a show or downtown. Remember that he is an individual and, as such, has his individual desires, separate and distinct from your own desires. If he is unable to make an appointment on time, don't make him feel that he is hurting you. Tell him that if it's essential that he be late or that he will be unable to make the appointment, then go ahead, you'll find something with which to while away the time. But don't, under no conditions, don't make him feel that because of him, you are suffering. He will never forgive you for it because he will not be able to forgive himself. It will prey on his mind and, eventually, it will turn out to be one of the factors of demolishing his love for you. If he likes to go to a ball-game, try to teach yourself to like the game so that, when he returns, you will be able to talk intelligently to him about it. If, on the other hand, your girlfriend enjoys the ballet, don't make fun of her enjoyment.

Ask her intelligent questions about what she has seen. Try to understand her likes and, if possible, adapt them to yourself. It is well known that the tethered dog yearns mightily for the roving alleys. Given his freedom, he returns after a few hours "dragging his tail behind him," hungering for the touch of his master's hand, his master's love and especially his master's food. Love is a kind of food and your wandering Charley who is seeing the fights will be sure to return to you anxious for the embrace of your arms, the touch of your fingers and the feel of your lips. With these always present, he will resent them in time and yearn for the ballfield, the fight ring or the poolroom and, you may be sure that if he can't get to them with your knowledge, he'll do it secretly and thus, begin, what must eventuate into a broken up love affair. Don't ever be possessive. If you want to have don't hold too firmly.

MESSAGES OF LOVE

This naturally opens up the question of love letters. When you are separated from your loved one either because of a business trip or otherwise, an ideal manner of bridging the distant gap that separates you from your lover is the love letter. Oh, I know that most men consider it effeminate nowadays to write mushy, gushy love letters but they are absolutely essential. I don't mean to infer that they should write mush. No, but they can write a letter to a distant loved one that can reassure her that she is always in his mind, that he looks forward intensely to the time when he will meet her again and that she is still the only one in the world as far as he is concerned. The imagination is powerful in human beings.

We can build and create where nothing actually exists. And distance aids the imagination. A woman or a man might imagine the most preposterous of things if she has not seen her loved one for some time. A love letter can rectify all that.

In writing a love letter, try to imagine that your loved one is seated next to you on the sofa and that you are whispering sweet nothings into her ear. Then, instead of speaking those things to her, write them down on a paper (never typewrite them because type is too impersonal for as personal a missive as a love letter). Don't write the letter as though it were a guidebook. Don't be too brief. Go into complete detail about the things you've done and seen. And try, always, when possible to connect up those things with something parallel that happened to the two of you. I mean that if you happen to see a particularly gorgeous sunset, describe it and then mention that it made you think of the time you both went down to the Dunes and saw that marvelous sun setting in the west.

A perfect love letter that I once read went as follows:

```
Darling Anne:

Have I ever told you I love you?

Well, tonight, as I sit here in my lonely ho-
tel room a thousand miles away from you, I begin
to realize why it is that I love you. I begin to
realize how all important you have become to my
happiness. I begin to realize that distance does
not lend enchantment but it really makes for un-
happiness.

Have I ever told you I love you?
```

I go to the beach and, immediately, I remember the happy times we had together at Clarendon, particularly that night when we found that poor little kid crying because he was lost and we took care of him the while we imagined that be was our own little boy. Remember? I go about my business here, talk about "carpet tacks and sealing wax" but, in my mind, there is only the picture of a little girl with dark brown hair and big black eyes and with two quivering lips that almost make me want to drop everything and rush back home to her. But, no, I force myself to remain and try to sell "carpet tacks and sealing wax" so that we can save enough toward that little cottage in Elmwood we've talked so much about.

Have I ever told you I love you?

Darling, take care of yourself. I'm in perfect health and just raring to go. How are the folks home? (*Here, if you have children, enquire of them and perhaps, mention some little quirk of theirs'.*) The orders are coming in much better than I expected which means that, soon, I'll be flying back to you and to happiness.

Have I ever told you I love you?

                    Your darling,
                         Gray

You get the idea from this letter. Gray informs his darling Anne that she is always on his mind. With a clever little device, he tells her that he loves her ever and ever. He recalls the scene of one of their complete hours of happiness at the beach. He brings up a little secret intimacy (the Elmwood cottage) and with it creates a point of contact with her that is secret to themselves alone. He tells her that business is satisfactory without overburdening his letter with weighty details. Even though he may have had a slight attack of indigestion, because of the change of food, he does not mention it for fear that he might upset her. After all, there's no sense in having her worry unnecessarily about him a thousand miles away.

THE GREEN-EYED DRAGON

This leads into a discussion of that bugaboo of lovers, that awful green-eyed monster of a bugaboo, jealousy. If you want to lose your lover, the easiest way to accomplish the deed is to make him jealous. La Rochefoucauld once said that "The more we love the nearer we are to hate." And you will discover that fact to be true the minute you have reason to make your loved one jealous. For, what was once an intense love will be turned to an intense hatred. It takes very little to change love to hate and jealousy is a powerful factor in doing it. But jealousy, on the other hand, need not be a reason for breaking off love if the person who is jealous is able to reason to himself and realize the basis of his jealousy.

First, a jealous person should realize to what extremes his jealousy can lead him. He should always remember what that poet meant when he wrote:

> —*JEALOUSY,*
> *That wedlock's yellow sickness,*
> *That whispers separation every minute.*

And that is what jealousy leads to, separation. Yet, if you have any sense at all, you can very easily talk yourself out of jealousy. If you are a woman and your lover seemingly has cast his eyes in the direction of a particularly attractive woman and comments on her beauty, there is no need for you to sulk in a corner and weep and grow wrinkles. Realize that there are thousands of other women more beautiful than you. But also realize that he, your lover, had found you attractive enough to fall in love with you. With this realization, strive the harder to make yourself more attractive to him. Make the most of the qualities that you have. If the other woman is gorgeously shaped but has dishwater hair, the while your hair is a beautiful bronze, say to yourself, "huh! but did you see her hair! Nothing like my hair!" Then remember what Oscar said the last time he smelled of your hair and ran his fingers through it and marvelled at its length and color and luster and sheen. All of these things will serve to re-channel what was once jealousy into self-appreciation. And the more appreciative you are of your own charms the more those charms will become evident to your loved one. If you are a man, don't create suspicions of lost love in yourself when you see Elsie talking animatedly to another man, Charley Frith, perhaps, who was the star halfback at Yale. Charley may be an athlete but, being human, he has his faults. Realize that just because Elsie is in love with you is no sign for her to be totally unattracted to somebody else. Usually, such jealousies are the result of a feeling of inferiority in the person who is jealous. If such is the case, as it usually is, then you should strive to overcome that feeling by improving yourself. Use your jealousy as a lover of self-improvement. But, whatever you do, if you are jealous, don't let it be known. Hide it from everyone and most of all from your lover. She may be the kind who feels that, in making you jealous, she is proving to herself that she is still attractive to other men besides yourself. Realize that she is only kidding herself. Realize also that, just as she has found charm in another male, so have you found charm in other women. Don't kid yourself. You know well enough that a pretty leg on another woman can attract your attention away momentarily from your lover. Then realize, too, that an attractive young man can distract the attention of your lover from you to him. But, remember, that such things are comparatively short-lived. They are only incidental. It is your love for her and her love for you that will last forever and ever, providing it is given the opportunity to do so. You know, as the poet knew that:

> *The world is cold and death is everywhere.*
> *I turn to you, and in my heart's despair*
> *Find peace and rest. We know, through foul and fair*
> *That love is sweet.*

Wait, bide your time, allow the jealous feelings to wear off and, before you know it, she will be back in your arms finding "peace and rest" "through foul and fair" and knowing that with all the heartaches and pain, with all the tortures and torment, with all the bitterness, "love is sweet."

And the same applies to lover's quarrels. Usually, they begin with little things. And, gradually, from this little difference grows a bigger difference until, finally, the quarrel results in separation. Say to yourself, "Do I really want to lose her?" in the middle of a quarrel. Think of how empty life would be without her. Think of the loss you would sustain, without being able to see that funny little crinkle in her eyes when she smiles. Think of how devoid life would be of all happiness were you never to be able to feel her warm, passionate lips against your own. Think of all these things which will be denied you if you break up, while you are quarreling and, soon enough, you will wisely give in to her (or to him) and, once more you will be lovers again, your arms will be around her, your lips will be on her's, and "all will be right with the world." Then will be the time for you to think of that beautiful poem:

> How would I then be loved? Devoted
> Of all the world I must be first and best
> And fill the measures of existence full
> For him whose heart and mine do interchange.
> Devotion, patience, tenderness—no more
> Could human heart desire this side of heaven.

CHOOSING A HUSBAND OR WIFE

This is a difficult subject of which to write. Because choosing something indicates that you use reason and logic in making your choice and, unfortunately, love is devoid of either. When a girl falls in love with a man, her action is the direct result of an emotion and not a thought. Because love is entirely emotion and entirely irrational. Therefore, it is for this reason that the utmost of care must be taken to be certain that the person with whom we fall in love is the proper person, the sort of person with whom you can expect to live happily the rest of your life.

If you are one of the fortunate few who are able to reason before you react to an emotion, then you will give this subject considerable thought and, no doubt, your love life will be a happy one. But if you are the kind that falls in love first and thinks afterwards, as most of us are, then you must not allow your love affair to continue too long before you sit down with yourself to reason your situation out. You must be certain, absolutely certain, that your lover will make a proper mate for you.

KNOW THYSELF

The first thing you should ask yourself is do you know yourself? Recognize your faults as such and your virtues. Don't exaggerate or minimize either. Once you understand yourself you will be able to understand what you will need to make yourself happy. With that knowledge, you will be able to judge your loved one rationally with the purpose of determining whether he or she can make you happy. Ask yourself, is that person able to give and receive the good with the bad just as you should be able to give and receive? If you can truthfully answer "yes" to this question, if your answer is based upon facts and experiences, then you can go onto the next question.

TWO OF A KIND

Have the two of you sprung from the same strata of life? In other words, are you physical, mental and economic equals? Are your religious differences sufficient to make married life a continual round of religious arguments and bickerings? Are they powerful enough to split you when you are married and have children because you cannot agree as to how the children are to be brought up? Think also of your families: will they be able to get along with each other? Oh, I know, you're not marrying his family, you're marrying him. But you're just being an ostrich because, being his family, they still have a powerful hold on him, if he is any sort of a man at all. It may make romantic reading for a prince to fall in love with a peasant girl but, you may be sure, for the couple, it will not make romance. The couple has nothing common except their supposed love for each other and you can't very well live on love alone, although a lot of us seem to think we can. History has taught us that this disparity of stations can result only disastrously in a dissolution of love. Lord Byron married a rich commoner and lived to regret his rash act. Bulwer-Lytton married a girl below his position and got a shrew who made his life miserable for him. Keats fell in love with a waitress and suffered agonies of torture. George Gissing fell in love with and married a prostitute and left her for another lowborn woman whom he left after a short while. The French poet, Baudelaire, loved and married an illiterate negress and, from that time on, became the most morose and despondent of French literary men. The world is full of similar examples and the cases in which such a mixed marriage turned out happily, such as when John Howard married his nurse and when Peter the Great married a peasant girl who later turned out to be one of Russia's finest rulers, are exceptions which serve only to prove the rule. And that rule is to marry neither above or below your station.

COME DOWN TO EARTH

This leads into another rule because it is a natural followup of the preceding one. Are you certain that the man you love will make an ideal companion? There is a vast difference between love and companionship. Love is lived on the highest plane. Companionship is lived on a lower plane. And you cannot live continually in the higher, more rarified, more frenzied atmosphere of love all your life. Most of the time you've got to come down to earth and that ability to come down to earth and live with your loved one depends on whether you are good companions. The prime necessity for an ideal companionship is not that the two temperaments should be exactly alike but that they should be able to blend perfectly. It isn't necessary that everything be in common between the pair. But it is essential that there should be enough things in common, enough things which you can enjoy to make for a congenial companionship when passionate love is held in abeyance. As the poet put it, it means:

> *Happy the youth who finds a bride*
> *Whose heart is to his own allied—*
> *The sweetest joy of life.*

One thing to avoid, and this injunction is made mostly to women for it is they who attempt this impossible task: don't fall in love with a man whose faults you recognize but which you hope to eradicate by reform. You can't reform anyone. Reform means change and if you change the man you love, you are more than likely to change not only him but his love for you. This reform requires constant nagging and the most efficient way of losing a man's love is to nag him about his faults.

FAULTS AND VIRTUES

Naturally, in choosing a mate, it is imperative that he or she be healthy. The ailing woman is a menace to any love affair. She should be strong enough to do housework, she should be strong enough to bear children, she should be strong enough to do the work necessary toward the building of a home. Again, the same should apply to the man, but even more so, for he is going to be the main support of the future family. Upon him and his strength will rest the job of earning the expenses. And if he is unable to do so because of ill-health, the future of the love-match is put in jeopardy. Money is a very important factor here as it is in practically everything else. And the young girl, before she falls in love with a young man whose intentionals are serious, as they should be, should make herself doubly certain that he will be able to take care of her and himself after they are married. Money has been called the root of all evil; certainly it is the root of evil in a married life. More marriages have been wrecked by money problems than, perhaps, by any other single factor. Therefore, it is also necessary that the young man sees to it that his future wife is not extravagant, that she realizes the work that goes toward the earning of his salary, that she is economical in food, dress and luxuries.

$$1 + 1 = 3$$

You may ask: what has all this to do with love? The trouble with lovers is that, immersed in their world of love, they cannot seem to realize that others exist in the world besides themselves and that there are other things to do, in a lifetime besides making love. If these other things are neglected, slowly but surely, they will burrow insidiously into the love life, undermine it by gnawing at the foundations and, in a very short time, effect a collapse of the whole structure of marriage. These injunctions are necessary because they will lead the way to permanence, a permanence of the love life. And the only way to assure them of this permanence is to build for the future. When you are in love, ask yourself whether there is anything about the character of your mate that might injure your relationship in years to come. If you can truthfully and honestly say "no" to this question, then you will have before you a lifetime of happiness such as the most richest of millionaires has never experienced. You will be assured of the company of a woman who is all things in one; wife, companion and mother to your children. You will have built yourself a home that will be your castle, impregnable to the assaults of those malign forces that destroy a happy home. You will have, as the poet has written:

A bit of rock, and a light atop
Which flashes forth, as the shadows drop,
The smallest place in the world it seems,
Yet full of hope and full of dreams,
As any place more proudly blest;
For two, this tower—home is best.

NOTES

NOTES

NOTES

NOTES

NOTES

NOTES

NOTES